Under the Stars

by Nic Grant
illustrated by Melissa Iwai

HOUGHTON MIFFLIN HARCOURT
School Publishers

Copyright © by Houghton Mifflin Harcourt Publishing Company

All rights reserved. No part of this work may be reproduced or transmitted in any form or by any means, electronic or mechanical, including photocopying or recording, or by any information storage and retrieval system, without the prior written permission of the copyright owner unless such copying is expressly permitted by federal copyright law. Requests for permission to make copies of any part of the work should be addressed to Houghton Mifflin Harcourt School Publishers, Attn: Permissions, 6277 Sea Harbor Drive, Orlando, Florida 32887-6777.

Printed in Mexico

ISBN-13: 978-0-547-42694-5
ISBN-10: 0-547-42694-1

2 3 4 5 6 7 8 0908 18 17 16 15 14 13 12 11 10

If you have received these materials as examination copies free of charge, Houghton Mifflin Harcourt School Publishers retains title to the materials and they may not be resold. Resale of examination copies is strictly prohibited.

Possession of this publication in print format does not entitle users to convert this publication, or any portion of it, into electronic format.

See the sun.

See how orange it is.

See the moon.
See how white it is.

See the star.
See how bright it is.

See the sky.
See how starry it is.

zzzzzzzz

Responding

WORDS TO KNOW Word Builder

Ask a question about things you can see in the sky. Use the word "how" in your question.

Write About It

Text to World Draw a picture of things in the sky. Label each thing in your picture. Then use vocabulary words to tell about the picture.

how | **is**

Stop to tell important ideas as you read.